EXERCISE BOOK

FOR

DR. HENRY CLOUD'S
WHY I BELIEVE

_____
_____

© COPYRIGHT 2024 – All rights reserved

The content contained within this book may not be reproduced, duplicated or transmitted without direct written permission from the author or the publisher.

Under no circumstance will any blame or legal responsibility be held against the publisher, or author, for any damages, reparation, or monetary loss due to the information contained within this book, either directly or indirectly.

LEGAL NOTICE:

This book is copyright protected. It is only for personal use. You cannot amend, distribute, sell, use, quote or paraphrase any part, or the content within this book without the consent of the author or publisher.

DISCLAIMER NOTICE:

Please note the information contained within the document is for educational and entertainment purposes only. All effort has been executed to present accurate, up to date, reliable, complete information. No warranties of any kind are declared or implied. Readers acknowledge that the author is not engaged in the rendering of legal, financial, medical or professional advice. The content within this book has been derived from various sources. Please consult a licensed professional before attempting any techniques outlined in this book. By reading this document, the reader agrees that under no circumstances is the author responsible for any loses, direct or indirect, that are incurred because of the use of the information contained within this document, including but not limited to errors, omissions, or inaccuracies.

THIS BOOK BELONGS TO:

_____

_____

_____

_____

TABLE OF CONTENTS

INTRODUCTION:
1. Welcome to the Journey
2. How to Use This Workbook
3. About Dr. Henry Cloud

Chapter 1:
The Basis of Belief
1. Defining Belief: According to you, what is "belief" and How would you distinguish between knowledge and belief?
2. The Significance of Belief in Our Lives - What makes belief significant in your life and How does your faith affect the choices you make every day?
3. Personal Reflections: What guiding principles influence your perspective? How have you changed your beliefs throughout time?

Chapter 2:
Evidence Gathering
1. Scientific Views on Religion: How does science confirm or refute your beliefs and Which scientific findings have affected your religious beliefs?
2. Philosophical Insights: Which arguments from philosophy align with your beliefs and How do you balance philosophical issues with your religious beliefs?
3. Testimonies and Personal Narratives: Could you describe an instance in which you sensed the presence of God?

CHAPTER 3:
Confronting Doubt
1. Comprehending the Nature of Doubt: What questions have you had about your faith and How do you address and interpret these uncertainties?
2. What is the source of your doubts and How do you suppose others handle doubts of a similar nature?
3. Techniques for Resolving Doubt: What approaches do you use to deal with and get past doubts and In what way might skepticism spur on a stronger faith?

Chapter 4:
Community's Impact
1. The Influence of Religious Communities: What role does your community play in shaping your beliefs and What part does a community of support play in your spiritual development?
2. Discovering Your Faith Community: What characteristics are you looking for in a faith community and In what ways can you be a part of and gain from a faith community?
3. Introspective Questions: Who are the main pillars of your faith community and How do you deal with the divergent viewpoints in your community?

Chapter 5:
Historical Scripture Reliability:
1. How Do You Judge Spiritual Texts' Reliability and Which verses hold the greatest significance for you?
2. What relevance do texts have for your own experiences and What fresh understandings have spiritual writings given you?
3. Reflective Questions: How do you apply the Bible to your day-to-day activities and Which verses in the Bible motivate and challenge you?

Chapter 6:
Supernatural and Miracles
1. Characterizing and Interpreting Miracles
   What do you think makes a miracle and What importance do miracles have in your worldview?
2. Individual Encounters with the Paranormal
   Have you been a part of or seen a miracle and What impact do these encounters have on your faith?
3. Thought-Provoking Questions
   How do you account for the happening of miracles and What impact do miracles have on your understanding of God?

Chapter 7:
Faith-Based Personal Transformation
1. Stories of Transformation: What positive effects has faith had on your life and Which inspirational tales of change motivate you?
2. The Process of Personal Growth: What aspects of your life have improved as a result of your faith and How do you keep working for personal development?
3. Reflective Questions: What challenges have you overcame because of your faith and How do you tend to and foster your spiritual development?

Chapter 8:
Realizing Your Beliefs
1. Practical Applications of Faith: How do you apply your faith to your day-to-day activities and What roadblocks do you encounter when following your faith?
2. The Influence of Faith on Everyday Life: How does your faith affect how you interact with other people and What part does faith play in the choices you make?
3. Reflective Questions: What concrete ways do you show your faith and Which aspects of your life most closely align with your core values?

CHAPTER 9:
Confronting Skepticism
1. Recognizing Skepticism: What are typical arguments made by skeptics against faith and What is your response to doubt?
2. Having Meaningful Conversations with Skeptics - What are some effective ways to have meaningful conversations with skeptics and What techniques facilitate polite conversations about faith?
3. Reflective Questions: Which skeptic arguments present the biggest obstacle for you and How do you strike a balance between faith and reason?

Chapter 10:
Maintaining Your Spiritual Path
1. Techniques for Increasing Belief
   What rituals assist you in preserving and enhancing your faith and How do you apply these exercises to your daily routine?
2. The Value of Ongoing Education - What are your methods for staying knowledgeable and motivated in your religion and What tools do you utilize to continue developing spiritually?
3. Reflective Questions: What are your plans for continuing on your spiritual path and How are you going to strengthen your convictions?

Results
1. Accepting Your Religious Path - What knowledge have you gained from this worksheet and In what ways has your understanding of faith evolved?
2. Dr. Henry Cloud's Concluding Remarks - Which of his main points really speak to you and How are you going to incorporate these lessons into your life?
3. Creating Your Own Personal Faith Declaration - What is your own personal creed and How will you apply this statement to your day-to-day activities?

CONCLUSION

NOTES

INTRODUCTION

You are about to embark on a journey that has the potential to transform your life, revitalise your spirit, and assist you in better comprehending your beliefs. Within the pages of this workbook, you will embark on a journey through faith that goes beyond the realm of basic academic research and into the heart of one's own inner conviction. The profound perceptions of Dr. Henry Cloud serve as the foundation for this.

Embracing Your Own Spiritual Profession

A journey, a desire for meaning, and a profound connection to something that is greater than ourselves are all components of true faith. In reality, it is more than simply a notion. It is the intention of this workbook to guide you through a process that is both contemplative and illuminating, regardless of whether you are just starting out on your journey of discovering your beliefs or are trying to enhance a faith that is already very strong.

On what grounds do you have such a belief? The investigation that we are conducting centres on this subject. The answer to this question is one that delves into the most profound aspects of our lives, our hopes, and our humanity. Through the unique combination of spiritual knowledge and psychological understanding that he possesses, Dr. Henry Cloud offers a road map that will assist you in discovering and presenting your own solutions.

Relating to the physician Henry Cloud

As a well-known psychologist, leadership expert, and author of books that have sold millions of copies, Dr. Henry Cloud has committed his professional life to gaining an understanding of the mind and soul of individuals. Through his work, he bridges the gap between psychology and spirituality, offering a comprehensive approach to faith and personal development. Due to the fact that his ideas are founded on both centuries-old spiritual truths and scientific research, Dr. Cloud is able to provide advice that is both reliable and motivational.

Making the Conditions Necessary for Adjustment

By embracing the questions that lead to better understanding and transformation, rather than merely focusing on offering solutions, the purpose of this workbook is to have the reader embrace the questions. Throughout the course of your interaction with the information, you will be put to the test, inspired, and driven to explore deeper into your ideas.

What are you hoping to accomplish by the end of this experience? The purpose of this workbook is to provide you with assistance in accomplishing your goals, which may include establishing a more profound sense of purpose, gaining a more profound understanding of your values, or forming a more intimate connection with your community. You will be able to acquire a full and well-rounded understanding of your ideas with the help of each chapter, which is designed to build upon the one that came before it.

This is the beginning of your journey of faith.

Determine what you want to accomplish with this workbook as soon as you begin. What is it that you wish to discover about yourself and the beliefs that you hold? Could you tell me about the impact that you believe this trip will have on your life? Putting your thoughts down on paper and keeping them near at hand will help you to remember why you decided to go in this direction in the first place.

Thank you for joining me on this journey of self-reflection, education, and development. Welcome to the "Why I Believe" page that Dr. Henry Cloud has created. Now, let's get something going.

HOW TO USE THIS WORKBOOK

Approach this workbook with an open mind and a willing heart to get the most out of it. The following advice will help you go through the chapters and exercises:

1. Make Time – Allocate particular periods of time every week to complete the chapters. Maintaining consistency will enable you to stay focused and advance steadily.

2. Thoughtfully - Give each question and exercise your full attention. Think carefully about your responses and how they apply to your experiences and life.

3. Be Honest- Honesty is vital for growth. Be sincere in your reflections and opinions. You can safely explore your true self in this workbook.

4. Implement the Teachings - Consider how you can use the knowledge and understanding from each chapter in your day-to-day activities. Enacting long-lasting changes requires practical application.

5. Ask for Assistance - Do not be afraid to ask friends, family, or members of your faith group for support if you are having trouble with any particular chapter. Sharing your journey can provide new insights and encouragement.

6. Maintain a Journal - Make notes of any further ideas, comments, and objectives on the notebook pages that are included at the conclusion of the workbook. This will enable you to monitor your development and gauge your progress.

7. Revisit and Reflect - Go back and review earlier chapters and reflections on a regular basis. As growth is a continuous process, looking back and reviewing your earlier reflections can offer fresh perspectives and validate your advancement.

Chapter 1:
The Basis of Belief

Chapter 1:
The Basis of Belief

1. Defining Belief: According to you, what is "belief" and How would you distinguish between knowledge and belief?

2. The Significance of Belief in Our Lives - What makes belief significant in your life and How does your faith affect the choices you make every day?

3. Personal Reflections: What guiding principles influence your perspective? How have you changed your beliefs throughout time?

Chapter 2:
Evidence Gathering

Chapter 2:
Evidence Gathering

1. Scientific Views on Religion: How does science confirm or refute your beliefs and Which scientific findings have affected your religious beliefs?

2. Philosophical Insights: Which arguments from philosophy align with your beliefs and How do you balance philosophical issues with your religious beliefs?

3. Testimonies and Personal Narratives: Could you describe an instance in which you sensed the presence of God?

CHAPTER 3:
Confronting Doubt

CHAPTER 3:
Confronting Doubt

1. Comprehending the Nature of Doubt: What questions have you had about your faith and How do you address and interpret these uncertainties?

2. What is the source of your doubts and How do you suppose others handle doubts of a similar nature?

3. Techniques for Resolving Doubt: What approaches do you use to deal with and get past doubts and In what way might skepticism spur on a stronger faith?

Chapter 4:
Community's Impact

Chapter 4:
Community's Impact
1. The Influence of Religious Communities: What role does your community play in shaping your beliefs and What part does a community of support play in your spiritual development?

---

2. Discovering Your Faith Community: What characteristics are you looking for in a faith community and In what ways can you be a part of and gain from a faith community?

3. Introspective Questions: Who are the main pillars of your faith community and How do you deal with the divergent viewpoints in your community?

Chapter 5:
Historical Scripture Reliability:

Chapter 5:
Historical Scripture Reliability:
1. How Do You Judge Spiritual Texts' Reliability and Which verses hold the greatest significance for you?

2. What relevance do texts have for your own experiences
and What fresh understandings have spiritual writings given you?

3. Reflective Questions: How do you apply the Bible to your day-to-day activities and Which verses in the Bible motivate and challenge you?

Chapter 6: Supernatural and Miracles

Chapter 6:
Supernatural and Miracles
1. Characterizing and Interpreting Miracles

What do you think makes a miracle and What importance do miracles have

Chapter 6:
Supernatural and Miracles
1. Characterizing and Interpreting Miracles

What do you think makes a miracle and What importance do miracles have in your worldview?

3. Thought-Provoking Questions
How do you account for the happening of miracles and What impact do miracles have on your understanding of God?

Chapter 7: Faith-Based Personal Transformation

Chapter 7:
Faith-Based Personal Transformation

1. Stories of Transformation: What positive effects has faith had on your life? Which inspirational tales of change motivate you?

2. The Process of Personal Growth: What aspects of your life have improved as a result of your faith and How do you keep working for personal development?

3. Reflective Questions: What challenges have you overcame because of your faith and How do you tend to and foster your spiritual development?

Chapter 8:
Realizing Your Beliefs

Chapter 8:
Realizing Your Beliefs

1. Practical Applications of Faith: How do you apply your faith to your day-to-day activities and What roadblocks do you encounter when following your faith?

2. The Influence of Faith on Everyday Life: How does your faith affect how you interact with other people and What part does faith play in the choices you make?

3. Reflective Questions: What concrete ways do you show your faith and Which aspects of your life most closely align with your core values?

CHAPTER 9:
Confronting Skepticism

CHAPTER 9:
Confronting Skepticism

1. Recognizing Skepticism: What are typical arguments made by skeptics against faith and What is your response to doubt?

2. Having Meaningful Conversations with Skeptics - What are some effective ways to have meaningful conversations with skeptics and What techniques facilitate polite conversations about faith?

3. Reflective Questions: Which skeptic arguments present the biggest obstacle for you and How do you strike a balance between faith and reason?

Chapter 10: Maintaining Your Spiritual Path

Chapter 10:
Maintaining Your Spiritual Path
1. Techniques for Increasing Belief

What rituals assist you in preserving and enhancing your faith and How do you apply these exercises to your daily routine?

2. The Value of Ongoing Education - What are your methods for staying knowledgeable and motivated in your religion and What tools do you utilize to continue developing spiritually?

3. Reflective Questions: What are your plans for continuing on your spiritual path and How are you going to strengthen your convictions?

Results

1. Accepting Your Religious Path - What knowledge have you gained from this worksheet and In what ways has your understanding of faith evolved?

2. Dr. Henry Cloud's Concluding Remarks - Which of his main points really speak to you and How are you going to incorporate these lessons into your life?

3. Creating Your Own Personal Faith Declaration - What is your own personal creed and How will you apply this statement to your day-to-day activities?

CONCLUSION

Last Words

When you finish this workbook, take a moment to reflect on the path you have taken. This has not been just a mental exercise, but a thorough exploration of the fundamentals of your views. Together, we have traversed the mountains of evidence-based faith, ventured through the valley of doubt, and discovered the oasis of personal transformation.

Embracing Your Spiritual Journey

This workbook is a call to critical thinking, introspection, and growth. You've looked into the sources of your beliefs, fearlessly faced your doubts, and discovered that scripture and community can be sources of strength. You've also learned how to recognise miracles in everyday settings and found practical ways to live out your faith.

What changes have you made? Give yourself some time to reflect on the personal growth you've experienced. Perhaps you now understand your beliefs more clearly, feel closer to your faith, or even feel like you have a new purpose in life. Whatever you discover along the way demonstrates your commitment to the endeavour and your openness to adapt.

Moving Forward with Your Tour

The completion of this workbook does not mark the end of your adventure. Faith is a lifetime journey that evolves with each encounter and epiphany. Here are some methods to help you continue to deepen your faith:

1. Stay Curious: Never stop questioning and analysing your views. You can better understand faith—a dynamic concept—if you are open to new perspectives and ideas.
2. Join the Community: Create a group of individuals that support and challenge you. A strong religious community can provide accountability and support as you grow.
3. Practice Every Day: Incorporate religious activities into your daily life, whether they be by reading scripture, praying, meditating, or performing deeds of service. You may keep your religion vibrant and alive by following these routines.
4. Reflect Frequently: Consider your trip. By keeping a record of your thoughts and experiences, you can monitor your spiritual development and gain understanding.

Your Personal Faith Declaration

One of the most powerful outcomes of the journey is your own personal religious statement. This statement encapsulates your core beliefs and serves as a guide for how you want to live out your religion. Here's how to word and use your statement of faith:

1. Reflect on Key Takeaways: Identify the most significant lessons you have gained from this workbook.
2. State Your Beliefs: Clearly and concisely outline the essential aspects of your perspective.
3. Integrate Your Values: Discuss how the principles that are most significant to you impact your faith.
4. Live by Your declaration: Base all of your everyday contacts and decisions on your declaration of faith.

The Final Words of Dr. Henry Cloud

Dr. Henry Cloud's knowledge has served as the basis for this workbook. His stories have touched you, his observations have made you think about tough subjects, and his practical advice has provided you with the tools to make real change. Remember what Jesus said at the beginning: faith is a process, not an outcome. It's about understanding, evolving constantly, and accepting the answers as well as the questions.

When you close this workbook, remember to carry the courage to never give up, the curiosity to never stop learning, and the compassion to share your journey with others.

A New Beginning

As this workbook closes, you will begin anew. It acts as a launchpad for a deeper, more significant spiritual adventure. Keep using the information you've learned, the questions you've asked, and the insights you've gained. Let your faith be a lighthouse to guide you through life's joys and challenges. From a life of never-ending learning, improved understanding, and strengthened faith, greetings. As you proceed on your quest, the only thing limiting your possibilities is your belief.
We are honoured that you have decided to go with Dr. Henry Cloud's "Why I Believe". Salutations to the never-ending journey of discovery and the transformative influence of religion.

NOTES

NOTE

NOTE

NOTE

Made in the USA
Coppell, TX
04 October 2024

38173328R00037